Summer River

Summer River

Poems by
Joan Alice Wood Kimball

Sketches by
Margot Kimball

Riverwood Books

2014

Poems copyright © 2013 by Joan Alice Wood Kimball and Iris Johnson
Illustrations copyright © 2013 by Margot Kimball and Nina Kimball

2nd edition – February 2014

Printed and perfect bound on an Espresso Book Machine by Nell Pepper at the Harvard Book Store, 1256 Massachusetts Avenue, Cambridge, Mass. Design and layout by Matt Johnson.

ISBN 978-1-62890-908-1

Riverwood Books
165 Thoreau St
Concord, MA 01742

For Bill, Nina, Andy and Margot
—JAWK

For my mother and my father, who made a home for us on that magical and remote island, long before the advent of cell phones.
—MK

Reading by Candlelight

Contents

Three poems are by Iris Johnson. The others are by Joan A.W. Kimball.

Hickory Pickery

Hickory Pickery berries for lunch.
Hickory Pickery berries for brunch.
Up above the great heron flew,
and down below fish in a school.

by Iris Johnson

Boathouse at Night

Introduction

The poems and illustrations that follow have their roots in a family camp on Hickory Island in the St. Lawrence River, where my husband Geoff and I summered with our four children Margot, Andy, Nina, and Bill.

What is it like at an island camp?

Visitors quickly overcome the shock of no running water, no cars, no TV! They take right to a hand pump in the kitchen, a boat at the dock, and the river for baths. They learn to canoe, run the small outboard, snorkel, and sail. At night: cards or board games or reading by solar lighting and candles.

Hickory Island is a mile long. It sits in the middle of the Saint Lawrence River, where the river resembles a lake, nine miles across. There are six families with houses on its 82 acres. At the up-river end, our camp has two sleeping houses, a kitchen-living house, and a workshop for tools and repairs. The kitchen house was once a boathouse, and that's why it has such a wide opening for the door: it's where a boat used to float in. How it was brought to our end of the island sixty-six years ago, pulled by horses across the ice, is a story for another day.

Joan Alice Wood Kimball
November 17, 2013

The Bank by Iris's Clearing

Hickory Island

The dusty sun that shone in that old barn
The smell of grass, and earth, and simple things
The taste of berries from the ancient farm
The sound of birds as crickets play their wings

We'll lie outside and listen to the waves
One million stars will pierce the crisp black sky
The subtle wind will play across your face
We'll watch as midnight boats go sailing by

As morning rises brilliant colors dance
The quiet is a music seldom heard
When silent ripples break the water's trance
And fire shatters from the water bird

Iris Johnson

This River Hill

I step from rock to rock at the water's edge.
Cold wind flutes across my ear.
My heavy shoes loosen igneous grains
to join their fellows on the beach
where bleached shells and pulverized granite
attend the river's offering—float of weed, bloat of bass,
coot feather, cola can propelled on wave's breath
through rocky shallows to the insatiable strand.

This island rock, this river hill
this eroded base of a mountain peak,
proof of epochal ordeal,
was once higher than Everest.
A mile-high glacier,
bent on decapitating the mountain,
grinding, scraping, with granite fingernails
clawed our tender Paleozoic stone.

Footprints won't last on this beach.
Damp scents of soaking roots curl along the shore to a low ledge.
Easy leg up, I walk the ancient slab that flaunts
its glacial streaks across the shelf.

What Indians walked this river shore long ago
whose ancestors left Africa heading East
across the Pacific, the Rockies, the Great Lakes,
to meet my forebears heading West from Africa
across Europe and the Atlantic
to fetch up on this river plain?

What boulders here in the St. Lawrence were dropped
by the glacier after scraping this rock rim?

Those humpbacked, outsize cobbles
clumped in a watery course, lurk
beneath the sky's reflection.
They're the bane of the keelboats.
I've bumped them myself
with my catboat's centerboard.

Now I wander rudderless
on the wave-dampened sand, wind-dried shale.
I hunt the glacier's longevous traces
and find its spoor on our Cambrian coast.
I am the rover, I am the witness
invoking the ghosts of ancestors and ice.

From West Point

Socked In

One mile of cloud
to steer through?
A trifling thing!
No matter that the fog
obscured our passage

from Hickory, our island,
to the dock on Wolfe Island.
Bill and his friends must catch the ferry on Wolfe
to make the trip to Kingston on the mainland
to play their semifinal baseball game.

I'd planned to orient
the compass needle with the chart
and aim the boat as if we slid
along a straight-cut railroad track.

Embarked,
we soon lost sight of land
and moved inside a silent tube of white
that held us as we skimmed the surface warily.
Bill, my son and catcher for the team,
followed behind in a small outboard.

We didn't know the same misleading
wall of white enclosed a freighter, its engines cut,
waiting for the shifting fog to lift,
not blowing its warning horn.

No object could we see to measure speed.
No sound to signal other life.
In time I sensed we'd journeyed
over-long in blinding white,
and hadn't spied the red of the buoy,
the buoy, which marked the way
to the larger island's dock.
Instead, we met the silent merchant ship
in the great ships' channel.
The hulk, and not a buoy,
loomed through billowing whiteness.
A great black blade,
a static sentry in a wall of milk,
and far above us, the disembodied prow.

Like a pilot's badge, my compass
had made me cocky, until, until
I saw I'd not allowed for declination,
this year's magnetic variation.
The compass needle was pointed
fifteen degrees *west* of north.

Glancing back, by chance,
we watched a shape receding
behind Bill's boat:
the very buoy we sought!

I turned hard to starboard.
Could I track the peeping form
in shifting mists?
And not lose Bill behind?

We lost, then saw the buoy,
a giant chess-queen
veiled...unveiled,
a tantalizing shape.
Gradually, slowly,
keeping Bill in sight,
we crossed the flickering gap

until at last at the buoy's side,
we saw solid features:
the trees and dock on Wolfe.

Windsurf Wonk

To skim o'er the waves while you stand
On a board with a sail does seem grand.
But a boardsailing ride
In light winds that subside,
Might force you to swim for the land.

Sailboats and Wild Goose Island

Meadow on Hickory Island

I stride out of pines into sunlight.
The red-tail's cry,
a sickle raking the sky,
sets undergrass whiskers
quaking.

I finger spikes of purple vervain,
sense ear-taunting rustlings,
inhale thuriferous milkweed,
part the rasp-edged brush,
swallow raspberries
tart on the tongue.

Give me a year
to haunt this clay,
to brood, to question,
to pour seed pearls into hourglass cases
that measure the movement of earthworms
who haunt the burrows of weasels—
weasels who stare from tree roots on banks
overlooking the river
bearing fish
to the sea.

Line 8: *thuriferous* means "incense-bearing." It is derived from the word
thurible, the container that burns incense. The person who swings
the thurible is called the thurifer.

Meadow's Edge

Mink

Sandstone ledge at
water's edge: the place
to skin the perch
I've caught.

Mink swaggers past.
Leers at me.
Each white tooth made
for trapping dinner
in vise-clenched theft.
Mahogany hairs, deep
as summer grass,
invite my thumb.

Above its stretching neck,
jet-berry eye scoffs at me:
"What puny flesh you poke."

Tail straight, all business.
Short legs at river's edge.
The crouch. The plunge.
It shoots the swell—torpedo parting glass.

Few creatures question its muscle, its musk.
I must sharpen my knife.

Mink

Floating

Bathe in daylight on a wide and idle river,
eight feet above a glacier-planted boulder
steeped in mud that once was shell and fin.

Roll on your back to consider the blue scrim
that hides a four light-year span
to the nearest fixed object overhead.

What is truly fixed? The boulder?
The muddy dead?
The star?

Swim away from the bank.
Float free of earth's arcade.
Drift in Lethean water.

Ignore for once the fractious land
and cloud shadows that hump
across the ripples.

Otter's Claim

Below the dock
we spot a mound
of shells wave-winking
from the river mud—
an otter's winter forage.

We'd left the bay
before November's
horizontal winds could harry us
and dash our boat
against the ice-clad cleats.

The creature must have
scavenged far
along the ragged bottom
to snatch its fare
and shuck these nacreous lids.

Many frost-white mornings
it must have climbed
fur dripping
mussel in mouth

to sit here upon the wharf
skim these husks,
sample the empty
riverscape.

Skiff House and Dock

Two Geese

Two geese
yapping non-stop
flying low
over wind-wracked water

Paired for life
this old-wing couple
heading for Florida
bitching about the trip

"Why go so early
we'll hit the hurricanes"

"Flap it up can't you"

"Too many tourists
let's wait a month"

"Let's not"

And so on until they're out of sight

Cold October

Cold October made four hairy bees
Soporifically lie at their ease,
Each apparently dead
On a thistle-stem head,
Until warmed in the sun by degrees.

Bees on Thistles

Fish

Listen, there was a time
when I fished for sport.
I'd catch a dozen perch,
peeling the skin off
in a single piece.
I loved the mossy smell,
the emery-rough scales.

But I can't catch fish,
ever since Andy's whistling line
reeled in that leaping black bass,
scooped into my net.

It was scarred about the lips,
scales missing on its flank,
tournament size, gasping.
Eat it later, we agreed.
We kept it alive overnight.
At dawn over dewy grass
I stepped up to the tank.
See, the bass stirred,
tipped its eye at me.

I carried the creature
to the water's verge,
floated it on my palms,
until it tipped itself
into the flow.

A few days later,
Harold pulled up
in his aluminum boat
with three rods,
minnow pail,
fish box, lunch.

He hauled his fatigues
onto our dock and up
the hill, puffing a bit.
From a frothy beer
out bubbled his stories
of pike fishing,
duck shoots.
He was hunting
old river photos
to give to the museum.
Did we have any?

You know, Harold often
fishes off our point.
I shared with him our tale
of Andy's catch:
the large, battered bass with the
scratched-up mouth.
Harold gazed out the window.
"I know that bass...
I've caught it myself."

Photos by Nina Kimball, 1978

Catboat

Even though I held the tiller tight
to keep the little sailboat's bow upwind,
the craft, that untrustworthy "cat," just grinned.
It side-slipped on the swells, without the least

response to my steady, futile fight
to keep its heading straight, its one sail trimmed.
I, skipper, unaware it wasn't the wind
or waves, pressed hard to lee to set it right.

This boat I'd rescued, committed to the light
from years discarded in the woodland dim,
appeared to go its separate way on whim.
Just now I turn to catch a startling sight:

the plywood centerboard that should have hung
beneath the hull to keep the course direct,
its layers adrift, unglued from gross neglect,
is floating like a flag, a kite unstrung.

Thus, like an owner, grabbing for the leash too late,
I'll accept the wayward cat's defection.
I squint ahead, plotting a new direction
and end my useless fight to dominate.

Tiller and sheet in hand I alter course;
allow the roving craft to head downwind.
Landing at a neighbor's dock, chagrined,
    I admit, for sailing trips, my cat is boss.

Swimmers Supine

Swimmers supine in dark eye shades
Bas relief on wooden planks
Laughing loon

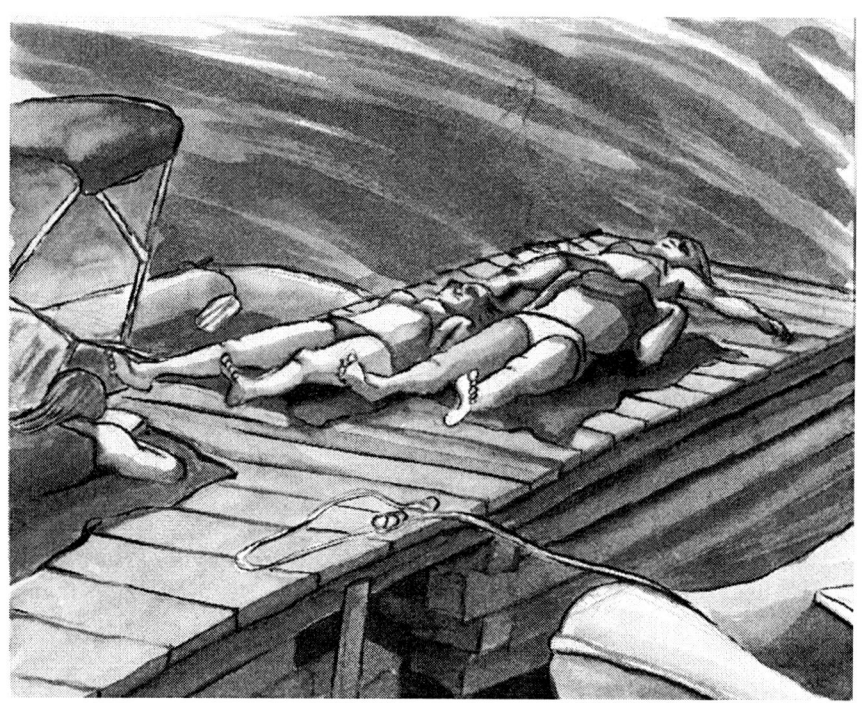

River Canvas

Now I will do nothing but let colors limn the tale.
I see pigments gossiping: soft, hard-edged, dark or bright.
The spin of the weathervane marking the wind,
pom-poms of trees, quick-marching waves, greetings of boats.

I see the ar c of the fisherm an's fling, the s ure leap of children aft er
    frogs,
the flash of a pike cadging mayflies, the shadow of a bass guarding his
    young.
The great blue heron w ith one leg lifted, its marble eye stalking a
    meal.
The chestnut hairs on a mink s lipping into the curr ent, the silver
    wake of her tail.

I see the sharp-angled wings of gulls as they glide under clouds.
On a branch over water the strut of a white-collared kingfisher.
A sentence of merganser ducklings, black letters teasing our eyes.

I see the cliff-face flaunting the scarlet bells of the windflower.
On the beach, the green of wild mint. In the gray rock pool, p uffs of a
    redwing bathing.
I see the wrack of the undertow when waves pull back, foaming white,
    the water from Niagara Falls, ever-born.

Light, shadow, color, shapes spreading from a vanishing point.
Sky, water, land—mind, retina, hand.

Herons over Field

Sun-gold

Sun-gold edge
to weeping willow leaf...
brief, airy dance!

Willow

Rhymes from a River

A stream so full a swamp seems dry,
A dawn, a golden scar.
A chain of mallards drifting by,
A chain of geese afar.

A willow shading bloated spill
Above a quick mink's wake.
A tethered rowboat not quite still,
A glint of water snake.

A tree crown shading early light,
A red root sucking mud.
A sap vein coursing its full height
Above the river flood.

A human touch, the dock protrudes,
An angle thrusting out,
A wooden stage for solitude,
A span to nurture doubt.

After Christian Wiman

No Anchor

a daylong paddle
a cloud-grilled sky

from time to time I lean
to see my face in the water

my lungs are silent trumpets
calling the communal fish

I choose this or that beach
I find a bleached skull, leave a mark

sandy feet feel the wave's grasp
never the same sand

never the same stream
I slake my thirst on messages of rain

Willow Tree with Canoe

Worker

Sporadic migrant
bobs on come-on petals,
shops for flower sugar,
shakes profligate pollen.

To this undocumented forager
I grant amnesty
to fertilize
my wild berry crop
with copulating dust,
then leave,
legs spore-laden,
a taste of ambrosia
on her tongue.

Raspberry Flower

Ode to a Storm

My skin is the rain
My eyes are the flood
My hands let go
My soul is free
My heart is open
Like the heavy clouds
And nothing matters
But the storm

The fierce wind
The unceasing waves
The steady ground
Beneath my feet
The pelting rain
The jagged rocks
And all around me
Is ocean

I can see myself
In the darkened sky
In the beaten grass
In the crashing waves
In the flooded valley
That leads to the beach
In the power of the wind
In the silence of the earth

I can see myself
In the boundless ocean
That flees to the sky
From the churning waves
Washing the land

With a thousand streams
And running back
Through swollen rivers

Your nourishing rain
Your destroying wind
My tiny life
Within your power
You are my soul
You are my blood
So soak my parched heart
Like the land before me
Because nothing matters
But the storm

by Iris Johnson

Birch Grove in a Wind

Late September

I clutch summer
 here—alone
on Hickory Island
in the middle of the river
nine miles wide.
No grandkids here
 this late in the year.

 A chill walk
past hoar-silver milkweed.
A bee sleeps on purple thistle
a deer with a ripped-sheet snort
 clears the field in leaps
slide show of
 foxes, wild turkeys
 migrating jays.

Fox

After a foggy night
 the final scene:
Wednesday morning wind
 and time to leave.

 I unplug the phone
from its charge on the solar battery
pocket it
lock the empty house
screw shut the propane tank
toss my two bags into
the motorboat hitched at dockside.

Turkeys

It's then I notice
the boat's dew-blurred windshield.
It will clear as I drive out.
   I think.

   The boat gallops into windy water
begins the five miles to the mainland.
   The canopy of trees
   recedes.

   I drive—leaning out the side to see—
      (I'll have to clear
      the windshield fog)
Yesterday's shirt will do for a towel.
   I dig it from my bag.

   Changing course
I head the boat to a low dock
on already-closed-for-winter Watch Island.
I jump onto the dock, shirt in hand,
tie the wind-hassled stern to a cleat
with the stern line,
rein in the bow with the bow line
   ready to cleat it,

Hickory House in a Storm

when a C-minor chord clarinets
over the skirling gale.

I quick-stamp on the restive bow line
palm the music from my pocket,
press the green key,
cover my ear.
Daughter speaks
five hundred miles away.
    Can I baby-sit there
    tomorrow at three?
        Yes!

 With windshield shirt-dried,
I rev the motor
pack into chop.
Angling through breaking seas
I head for winter
wind blowing eyelashes
    spray wetting cheeks.

    Under cantering clouds,
the boat's wake follows an eagle
as it banks and planes back
    toward the empty horizon.

Rainbow and Waves

Boat and Two Minks

Notes

Page 14 "Floating"
The nearest fixed object overhead would be our nearest star, Proxima Centauri, 4.24 light-years distant. It is seen in the southern sky, so it might not be overhead for this swimmer. Sirius, in the northern sky, is 8.4 light-years away. It would be interesting to consult an astronomer, though who's to worry?

Page 15 "Otter's Claim"
The shells shucked by the otter sparkle under water because of their nacre, the mother-of-pearl or *nacreous* lining of the shell. It is possible that, due to invasive species, large fresh-water mussels have disappeared from the upper St. Lawrence.

Page 17 "Cold October"
I've seen yellow and black bumblebees resting on thistles in October in the early morning on Hickory Island. Were they there all night? I don't know. It's not a new phenomenon, nor restricted to our continent. I've found 400-year-old testimony to the bees' preference for thistles in Shakespeare's "Midsummer Night's Dream," 4.1, lines 11-12. Bottom says to Cobweb, "Good monsieur, get you your weapons in your hand, and kill me a red-hipped humble-bee on the top of a thistle, and good monsieur, bring me the honey-bag." In the notes to the play, I find that the honey-bag is the bee's first stomach, which stores the honey the bee is gathering. Shuckard in his *British Bees* says "schoolboys often destroy the bee for the sake of its honey-bag."

Pages 18-19 "Fish"
Harold was our friend Harold Herrick, no longer with us, whose family still has a camp on a nearby island. In retirement he was a volunteer for the local museum and for Ducks Unlimited. *Andy* is Joan's son.

Page 22 "River Canvas"
Windflower is a local name for the wild columbine that chooses to seed itself at the land's edge, in the cracks of the rocky cliff, facing the sharpest winds of the north.

Acknowledgements

Thanks to the following journals for publishing some of the pieces in these pages.

The Aurorean 2004, "sun-gold"

Avocet 2004, "Meadow Walk," an earlier version of "Meadow on Hickory Island."

Avocet 2006 published an earlier version of "Otter's Claim"

Hawk & Handsaw 2013, "Fish"

Ibbetson Street 2012, "No Anchor"

Measure 2008, "Rhymes from a River"

Möbius 2003, "Separation," an earlier version of "Catboat"

Omnificent English Dictionary in Limerick Form 2006, "boardsailing" retitled "Windsurf Wonk"

Omnificent English Dictionary in Limerick Form 2011, "at one's ease" retitled "Cold October"

Thema 2004 published an earlier version of "This River Hill." After publication, I gave a copy to geologist Richard A. Young, in thanks for taking the family on a geological tour of the island, the tour that inspired the poem. In turn, he developed a photographic montage of island scenes for the text, and together we published it as a book in 2009.

Tower Poetry Anthology 2010, "Geese In September"retitled "Two Geese"

I was surprised and pleased to be able to match my island poems to drawings by my daughter Margot Kimball. Margot's daughter Iris Johnson contributed the poems *Hickory Pickery*, *Hickory Island*, and *Ode to a Storm*. My elder daughter Nina Kimball took the photos of her brother Andy that accompany the poem *Fish*. And my son-in-law Matt Johnson provided generous advice and guidance through publication.

Poetry mentor Tom Daley has inspired and encouraged my writing over the years. Four friends took the time to review the manuscript: Lorian Brown, Patricia Callen, Barbara L. Crane, and David Davis. Finally, I have learned much from the many colleagues in my poetry study groups.

—JAWK

muudful48@gmail.com

(914) 630-1344

woodkimball@gis.net

2011-Graf died
Spain· Madrid
Nina

About the Contributors

Joan Alice Wood Kimball has summered on Hickory Island in the St. Lawrence River almost every year since the age of six months. In her 70's she began publishing her poems, many about rivers. She continues with her children and grandchildren to walk the island fields and river shoreline every summer. Her online collection of published poems, Hand Delivery, is at http://handdelivery-joan.blogspot.com.

Margot Kimball is Joan's younger daughter. She is an artist living in Concord, Massachusetts. Her summers spent at Hickory Island on the St. Lawrence River have inspired much of her art.

Houses from the Water

Two Cedars

Illustrations

All but two drawings are by Margot Kimball.
The fishing photos are by Nina Kimball.